A CHANGE IN THE DARK

Poetry That Lights a Path

by

IKE TRIPLETT

Watersprings
PUBLISHING

A Change in the Dark by Ike Triplett
Published by Watersprings Publishing,
a division of Watersprings Media House, LLC.
P.O. Box 1284 Olive Branch, MS 38654
www.waterspringspublishing.com

Contact the publisher for bulk orders and permission requests.

Printed in the United States of America.
ISBN-13: 978-1-964972-00-8

Dedication

To Jesus Christ, my Savior.

The principle reason regarding who I am today.

If not for Him, I do not know where I would be.

To my father and mother who encouraged me to create this book. If not for them, this would merely have remained a concept that never came to fruition.

Contents

THE ARTIST I

ANGRY SEAS 3

DEVIANCY 5

OVER EXTENSION 6

EMPATHY 7

SCAR OF PERFECTION. 9

JUST A TOUCH II

2 X 2. 12

FLOORS THAT CRACK. 14

PRICE OF POWER, GIFT OF WISDOM. 16

LOVE. 18

FREEDOM 21

LIGHT OF THE SUN 23

A CHANGE IN THE DARK 26

DON'T WASTE YOUR TIME. 27

CONTINUING THE RESISTANCE. 29

SOMEWHERE BEYOND PERFECTION. 31

STAND DOWN. 32

THE ENTRANCE OF HOPE 33

THE OBVIOUS INEVITABLE. 34

SIT AND PLAY 35

UP IN SMOKE 36

TREKKING ALONGSIDE HOPE. 38

ABOUT THE AUTHOR 41

The Artist

Multiple rainbows on a single canvas
Each color is stroked beautifully between the clouds
Moving alongside the earth in orbit
Spinning
Spinning
Spinning
Embellishing the beauty of the sun
Intensifying its magnificence

But where does such artwork originate?
Patterns too intricate
Too detailed
To create themselves
An Artist is responsible
Who has the creative intelligence to produce such works of
    beauty?
Is it the same artist that designed the green forests?
Carved gigantic mountains that touch the surface of the sky?
The same being who dotted the stars in the dark infinity of space?

Everything must be His canvas
Mixing the correct colors together
Not too much
Not too little

The great Potter sculpted me perfect in His likeness
I am a vessel expressed in the portrait of the world
Only one in existence
But time after time, the world breaks me apart
But rather
I break myself
In a desire to become someone I am not
The Artist

Yet
He still restores me
While at the same time
Designing His
Magnum Opus
For all His compositions to be well secured
So I will never be broken again

Angry Seas

I sit in my boat
Quietly thinking my thoughts
I wait for fish
A storm arising
Mad seas start to escalate
My heart does the same
A whirlpool appears
Waiting to suck me inside
I mutter curses
My life starts to flash
I ponder the graven thought
To why I end here

....I remember now
I feel like a small infant
I...apologize
Instantly, it stops
I walk on land once again
But I'm not done yet
I go to my home

She is standing at the door

Tears still in her eyes

She is still angry

Will she be mine once again?

I pray that she will

Deviancy

Physical forms can fool the vision to believe what is underneath
Self-appointed judges scrutinize the skin based on what they see
When what is actually there doesn't correlate to their
    expectations, they retaliate

Deviancy from social norms can lead to uncertainty,
    misunderstandings, confusion, fear, and anger
The majority can reject it on the grounds that it is uncommon,
    therefore, unacceptable
The majority can tolerate it to an extent
Not the norm but it isn't deleterious to anyone
Whether people are accepting or not, the only thing that matters
    is the owner embraces the power

And changes the world for the better
While at the same time, induces similar individuals to do
the same

Over extension

There was a plant

A rose

With intricate petals developed, shoots up from the soil

Beautiful

With the sky etched with clouds held together by

The sun

It is the thing that it wants; the thing it needs

To be more beautiful

Flourishing above the others based on the mindset

of the mission

Determination

Continues to grow, continues to reach for the sun, and

giving everything to achieve it

Over extension

Of everything to reach the sun

Only to be burned down and washed away by the rain

Termination

Empathy

Sometimes true pain is in the agony of others
Listening to your cries pleading for it all to end
Seeing your trembling body
Your eyes are bulging
Red from tears
You attempt to mask your torture with a smile
I simply disintegrate
And neither of us have the knowledge to heal it
If I could pull back the tides of time
Reversing the hold it has on you within its waters, I would
Or at least I would try
Better than being helpless
Or seeing you so broken
Quite similar to witnessing someone
Becoming the newest resident of the house of Death while a
glass wall separates us
I can only sit there and watch you die
Slowly and painfully

With every thread and particle of my existence

I want to free you from total affliction

Instead I receive glimpse after glimpse

Of your convulsions every second I think about you

Echoes of your hurt

Happiness

Anger

Regret

All within me

But I have to remember that I cannot control what others feel

Only that I have the empathy to establish a connection

towards them

So they won't be alone in their struggle

Against the temptation to drift

Into the seemingly blissful abyss of death

Scar of Perfection

Counting to 100 with a sore throat
Some numbers come out
Some don't
Counting to a hundred life assessments with a quiver
Some I got right; some I got wrong
Over half of them wrong though

I stare precision in the face
I ask him if he is finished with me yet
Injecting me with his blood
Corrupting me to desire his nature
Perfection

All he does is laugh at my face
And laugh and laugh just like everyone else
I laugh too
The amusement of my failures
The sun favorably shines on them
Talent gleaming off their skin
Each breath they take in smells of intelligence

Excelling in everything and rising to the top of the world

While I'm alone on the ground

Alone with my failures kicking my cracked chest

One of the barriers to my heart broken

But that is not what hurts

Not what makes everything inside me disintegrate

Not the thing that completely paralyzes me in inner agony

The feeling that only death can sooth

It is the pain of knowing one can do something with

Everything

That he can muster

And watch it burn before his very eyes

Leaving behind a scar

    Forever reminding him that he could have done better

Just a Touch

Dying
I am losing myself
Was selfish one too many times
Was ignorant one too many times
Messed up one too many times
Made one too many people angry
Repeat

I drop to my knees on the concrete; there isn't any point
There is no value in this life
When I am constantly detrimental towards it
I see You midst the crowd
All I need is just a touch
To eradicate the infection sin has given me
By a love that will never leave me
No matter how many times I screw up

2 x 2

Love can't be copied

Only to be exhibited

Love can't always have a happy ending

Only to give others an opportunity to have one

The mind and body of a distinctive individual joins with another
and becomes one

$$1+1 = 2$$

Day after day, year after year eventually their love nurtures and
matures

$$2 * 2 = 4$$

But sometimes... the love is maltreated and divided

Souls dwindle and the bodies segregate back into the original

$$2 / 2 = 1$$

Already found someone else

The attempts to fill the void are forthright but inconceivable

The mind and bodies join with substitutes but will never incline
to the real thing

$$2 + 1 = 3$$

$$1 + 3 = 5$$

A CHANGE IN THE DARK

Drifting from each other for so long
They find nothing or no one to fill the hole so the love
    diminishes to nothing

$$1 -1 = 0$$

Floors That Crack

Floors that crack

Floors that creak

Are floors that are old

Trampled

Stomped

Such immense pressure placed on

You can still see footprints on the floorboards

Yet the floor remains

The walls that are built

Walls that glisten in the sunlight

Are walls that are strong

Nothing can get in

It can be seen as a means to keep things out to take over

the inside

Nothing can get out

A barren chamber within

Nothing else but the scraps of the goodness left

Perhaps the wall needs to be obliterated

Allowing the invaders to save them from themselves

A CHANGE IN THE DARK

The love that is made
Love that consumes hatred
Is love that is unstoppable
Has both mastered space and time
The conflict is its location
And who needs it the most?

Price of Power, Gift of Wisdom

I am power
The world is at my feet
With just a snap of my fingers
Everything changes to ashes
But I am stubborn
I don't know when to stop
Even if I do destroy the world
I destroy myself along with it

I am intelligence
Infinite information at my grasp
I know you better than you will ever know about yourself
So it's futile to fight me
But I am weak
I know too much
Even if knowledge is power
It is indeed a shame when
I am not in physical correspondence with
My knowledge

A CHANGE IN THE DARK

I am wisdom

I have power at the edge of my fingertips

But I also have enough insight to use it

So no one will die because of me

The combination is intense

Absolute power for ultimate change

Unlimited intelligence to know all the consequences for

those changes

With all these at my disposal

Where do I start?

Love

Love
It is a powerful thing
Only something I can feel
Never wanting to let it go

It enraptures me
Which can enhance my life
Or turn it upside down
Either way, I will never be the same

I do things in the name of love
Things I would never consider doing otherwise
I may even hurt others
To prevent them from hurting the one I love

Confused angels
Did not understand His journey
Did not understand why He left
He left a perfect world and entered an imperfect world

A CHANGE IN THE DARK

There is one purpose of His journey
Why He showed us His power
Why He told us of His wisdom
Why He demonstrated that death is just the beginning

Love...something that He has an abundance of
Seeing past our abundance of imperfections
The invaluable light that sacrificed itself
That someone like me would finally get the point

That His love never fails
In areas where I constantly struggle in
Such as abusing others for those whom I love
Including myself

Yet, He never participated in such hypocrisy
He has an all encompassing love
Containing those who both love and hate Him
Why else would he give Himself up to a people who did
not love Him?

I truly want to love others in the way He loves me
Not the selfish kind only reserved for people who will
return it
But rather the supernatural ability to give love to those
who truly need it
Even at the expense of my life

When I stand....
When I walk....
When I breathe....
I fervently desire to embody His love using every fiber of
my being

So when others see me
They do not see me
They see Your love
And want to know more about it

Freedom

Attempting to forget the effects of the war
The war you had with yourself
You were so hard to read
Closed and placed in a shelf

All the restless nights you had
Better than the dreams that choked your heart
You looked at the white dots in the dark abyss above
And wondered how you could be of such art

The canvas so beautiful
No judgment, double standards, nor pride
That annihilate your individuality
Killing your specialty
The qualities which people wanted you to hide

Not only were they hidden, they were broken
They couldn't seem to fathom that it wasn't meant to be
Found out too late that people aren't clay
Not meant to be changed and sculpted to what they wanted to see

You were crying in a cage lined with conformity

Starved of happiness refusing the condemnation that you were fed

I cry too

But the tears are of joy and relief

Because now

You are finally free

Light of the Sun

The land

Enveloped by the night

Night walkers roam across the land

Cannot see a thing of substance midst the shadows

Flailing our bodies

Continuing our existence chained to indifference

Lusting after power

Ignoring others to put ourselves first

Refusing to admit we are wrong

We simply live our lives as we please

A fellow night walker rammed into me

I severely educated it on the error of its ways

Hopefully it will not partake in such hatred again

That creature has the

Audacity

To claim I did the same to it

I shoved it away from me

Degenerate
And it falls
It falls
Falls
Into the void
Such pitiful creatures are we

A roar demolishes the endless night
Beautiful rays now shine in
Morning frees her from infinitely falling into the abyss
The era of the night walker is now over
It hurt at first
Blinding even
Then we quickly adapted to it
Having the ability to now see someone for who they are
And to see ourselves for who we are
Some strove to find some semblance of darkness to keep them
    comfortable
Willfully blinding themselves to the truth
For me, it was cathartic to actually see something
Beyond myself

Lilies now bloom within a magnificent valley

They spring upwards toward the rainbow stained sky

A glorious lion sits on the peak of a mountain

And the beauty has been magnified by

The Light of the Sun

A Change in the Dark

The little girl is in her bed crying
Praying that the dark will go away
Shadows at every corner
It still thinks it's in control
She is done crying now
Gets up from the floor
Walks through the door
Light in four
Three…two
One

Don't Waste Your Time

I must confess
I am a dreamer
When no one is around
Especially when overwhelmed
I do the impossible
I am fearless
Never was a coward
The earth is my throne
The moon is my footstool
This annoying thing called reality rings
Then I wake up

I know I'm not a single dreamer
We all have our impossible dreams
Only to be woken up by reality
You have the power to change that
The sky doesn't have to be the limit
You can soar through the stars

Slits change to bruises

Bruises mutate into scars

Ripples of blood invade a pond

The sacrifices we make

To show them something they never expected from

Me

A boy who just wants to prove his worth

But sometimes I

Or we

Lose ourselves in the process

But you're wasting your time

Being someone your heart isn't in sync with

To have intentions of being that one in a million

But we just burn ourselves out

Don't waste your time

For our time here is limited

Instead

Embrace your life

Continuing the Resistance

Continuing the resistance

Continuing the faith

Continuing the love

The war is already won

The enemy is down

The duty of the righteous soldiers is to keep the peace

Recruit new soldiers

Rescue the victims underneath the rubble

Do I understand?

Do I know that what's

Missing is my hand?

To write what is needed?

To fill the hearts of those that

The author concealed?

The silky, beauty on the outside

It changes our direction

Away from the blank, pained inside

IKE TRIPLETT

Please help me to accost
The meaning of who I am
And to write what's lost

And begin with a smile

Somewhere Beyond Perfection

A door leading to perfection
Is made of wood and lined with gold
A dove carved with an age before time was born
At least, that is what I'm told

I tried going in
I can't go in
No one can go in
Only trying to get your attention
You bring me in
Somewhere beyond perfection

Stand Down

You have me cornered

Nowhere to go

Bruised

Beaten

Cocked sniper aiming at its target

A speck of sweat rolls down my head

I drop to my knees

The enemy wants me dead

Craving to have that bullet through my skull

You smile to yourself

Thinking that my life holds by a thread that you hold

between your fingers

You ask of my final words

Expecting me to beg for mercy

Instead I get up and smile

Your weapons are useless

I already won

Because I was never alone

My answer?

Stand down

The Entrance of Hope

Tempests turn waters wild
Chaos smiles as she plays with her pearls of destruction
Lust licks her lips with an attraction to the pain
Along with Death who laughs at the burning flames
The worst part is that we opened our world to them

After years of struggling... I'm done
But that's when hope makes His entrance

The Obvious Inevitable

The inevitable is obvious to me
I see it every day
It reminds me every day
To stay in reality
My table is undoubtedly
Soaked in the high sky
It pulled me back when I was about to fly
But the inevitable to others aren't very free

The inevitable smothers some
Easier said than to deal with
The inevitable hurts some
Putting them in the room above
The inevitable does nothing to some
I pray it was a myth
To never learn to love

Sit and Play

When the future holds nothing I will sit and play
Memories of a better life consists of innocence and a naivety

While the world kills itself
I will sit and play
A game of happiness in a place where it will be not hard to
embrace my own self

When the eyes of the person I once knew turn against me in
anger without acceptance
I will sit and play
With my eyes signaling that my arms are always open

During the aftermath of the conflict
After what was accused and fought over for the sake of the battle
I will sit and play
Songs of truth to ascend me to my destination representing the
peaceful life that we all need
But never really want

Up in Smoke

Convince me I am wrong
Please tell me I'm wrong

That you can excuse me of the destruction
 But it's impossible to elude the condemnation

Can't you see the blood on my hands?
That have agonized this land?

Unconditional hatred
From the tears running down your bed

Hiding is not becoming
Of one who is hiding

In order to escape what you would do
Instead I'm waiting for you

To light the sparks and burn them away
Flames will consume the garbage and we will watch the smoke
    day to day

And smell the sweetness that will invade the atmosphere
 But for now I will wait here

In the dark knowing it will get better
So we can walk out into the light together

Trekking Alongside Hope

It is truly amazing
If one stops and starts thinking

About the evil this old world has been through
Including much more in the future he will brew

It seems one can only guess when
The next death due to the color of one's skin

Maybe next year, next month, today?
Perhaps it already happened, another urban tombstone on
display

It seems one can only guess the next act of terrorism
And it only leads to an increase of hatred towards all things
Muslim

We tend to put the entire culture in a frame
Surrounding a picture whose imagery consists of nothing
but blame

A CHANGE IN THE DARK

Or there will be a maker
The maker of a list of people who have been swallowed by
nature

This planet is falling apart
While issues surrounding famous people are taken more
close to heart

Ordinary man is exposed to so much, leading to the
introduction
Looks more like an increase now, of his desensitization

The accepting of this malicious curtain
Covering and deceiving the notion that good can never win

However, this is another solution
Another way to end this terrible situation

Get out of your way, your pride
Utilize yourself, your whole person as a guide

To a future in which frequently basks in light
Constantly being showered with love and everything that
is right

In order to begin to be within its scope

Is to walk alongside hope

Wanting to better yourself first in order to better the world

About the Author

Ike Triplett has been writing for as long as he can remember. Since around the age of four, he scribbled words together to communicate his desires, something he had difficulty speaking aloud. Over the years, he continued to express himself in written form, such as poems and short stories. Now, he writes not only for himself but for others as well. He wants his writings to inspire readers to think critically about their reading. He also hopes that readers will start critically analyzing the world around them to see things in a new light and how they can be rectified, especially in their own lives.